W9-BHX-710

The · Life Cycle · Series

The Life Cycle of a Wolf

Bobbie Kalman & Amanda Bishop

Illustrated by Margaret Amy Reiach

Crabtree Publishing Company

www.crabtreebooks.com

The Life Cycle Series
A Bobbie Kalman Book
Dedicated by Amy Reiach
For Mom, Dad, Stephen, and Michael—the pack that keeps me going

Editor-in-Chief
Bobbie Kalman

Writing team
Bobbie Kalman
Amanda Bishop

Editors
Niki Walker
Kathryn Smithyman

Copy editor
Jaimie Nathan

Cover and title page design
Campbell Creative Services

Computer design
Margaret Amy Reiach

Production coordinator
Heather Fitzpatrick

Photo researcher
Jaimie Nathan

Consultant
Patricia Loesche, Ph.D., Animal Behavior Program, Department of Psychology, University of Washington

Photographs:
Erwin and Peggy Bauer/Wildstock: front cover, pages 6 (inset), 10, 14 (bottom), 15, 16, 17 (bottom), 18, 20, 21 (bottom), 22-23, 24, 27 (bottom), 31
Tom Stack and Associates:
 Erwin and Peggy Bauer: page 9;
 Thomas Kitchin: pages 13, 14 (top), 30;
 Victoria Hurst: page 21 (top)
Robert McCaw: pages 7 (left), 8
Peter Crabtree: page 7 (right), taken at Schoenbrunn Zoo, Vienna (special thanks to Nicola Hill)
Other images by Digital Stock and Corbis Images

Illustrations:
All illustrations by Margaret Amy Reiach except the following:
Barbara Bedell: pages 5 (coyote and red wolf), 16, 29
Debi Fitzgerald: pages 1, 19

Crabtree Publishing Company
www.crabtreebooks.com   1-800-387-7650

Cataloging-in-Publication Data
Kalman, Bobbie
 The life cycle of a wolf / Bobbie Kalman & Amanda Bishop; illustrations by Margaret Amy Reiach.
     p. cm. -- (The life cycle series)
Includes index.
An introduction to the wolf, including some of the different types, pack structure, reproduction, hunting, and dangers faced by wolves in the wild.
 ISBN 0-7787-0687-7 (pbk.) -- ISBN 0-7787-0657-5 (RLB)
 1. Wolves--Life cycles--Juvenile literature. [1. Wolves.]
I. Bishop, Amanda. II. Reiach, Margaret Amy, ill. III. Title.
 QL737.C22 K36 2002
 599.773--dc21
                                                      LC 2002002277
                                                                 CIP

Published in
the United States
PMB 16A
350 Fifth Ave.
Suite 3308
New York, NY
10118

Published
in Canada
616 Welland Ave.
St. Catharines
Ontario, Canada
L2M 5V6

Published in the
United Kingdom
73 Lime Walk
Headington
Oxford
OX3 7AD
United Kingdom

Published
in Australia
386 Mt. Alexander Rd.
Ascot Vale (Melbourne)
VIC 3032

Contents

What is a wolf?

A wolf is a **mammal**. A mammal is a **warm-blooded** animal. Its body stays about the same temperature, no matter how hot or cold the air around it becomes. Every mammal has some hair or fur on its body. A wolf has a heavy coat of fur that keeps it warm. A female wolf gives birth to live babies. Babies feed on milk produced inside their mother's body.

The canid family

Wolves belong to the dog family *Canidae*. This family also includes coyotes, jackals, and **domestic**, or pet, dogs. There are three main **species**, or types, of wolves—red wolves, Ethiopian wolves, and gray wolves. There are many **subgroups**, or kinds, of gray wolves. All kinds of gray wolves do not look alike. Gray wolves that live in different **habitats**, or natural homes, have **adapted**, or changed, to suit their surroundings. The arctic wolf, for example, has shorter legs than those of other gray wolves. Its fur is often light in color, which helps the wolf blend in with its snowy home.

Scientists disagree

Many scientists disagree about how many types of wolves there are. Some scientists believe that red wolves, Ethiopian wolves, and gray wolves are three different species of wolves. Others believe that all wolves are gray wolves and that red wolves and Ethiopian wolves are two subgroups of gray wolves.

*Some scientists believe that the red wolf is a **hybrid**. They believe it has both coyotes and gray wolves as ancestors. A red wolf is smaller than a gray wolf but larger than a coyote.*

Until recently, scientists did not believe the Ethiopian wolf was a wolf at all. They thought it was a jackal. The Ethiopian wolf lives in the Simien Mountains of Ethiopia in Africa. It is about the size of a coyote.

Where do wolves live?

Wolves are found in the northern parts of North America, Europe, Africa, Russia, Asia, and the Middle East. In the wild, they live in various **habitats**, or surroundings. Wolves live in forests and deserts and on mountains, **plains**, and the **tundra**.

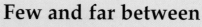

Most wolves live in this part of North America.

Alaska

Canada

United States

Mexico

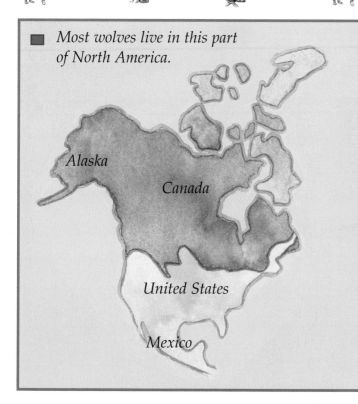

Few and far between

In the past, wolves lived in more places than did any other land mammal except humans. In North America, they lived from the Arctic to Mexico. Today, wolves are still found in many parts of North America, but most live in Canada and Alaska. The wolf populations in the United States and Mexico are much smaller. In fact, wolves are an endangered species in most regions of these countries.

This map shows the areas in which wolves live, but do not be fooled! There are only about 40,000 wolves living in all that space.

In the past, forests were the natural homes of wolves. Today, very few wolves can be found in wild areas.

In regions where wolves no longer live in the wild, some live in zoos, as shown above.

Part of a pack

The alpha wolves above survey the land, while their packmates below play in the snow.

Wolves live in groups called **packs**. Packs are made up of related wolves, usually parents and their **offspring**. Most packs have six or seven members, but some have more than twenty. The wolves in a pack live together and work as a team to hunt other animals.

Leaders of the pack

Wolf packs are led by a pair of wolves called the **alpha** male and female. "Alpha" is the first letter of the Greek alphabet, and it means "first." Alphas are usually the only wolves in a pack that have offspring. Younger wolves are less powerful, so they follow the leadership of the alphas.

Pack territory

A wolf pack lives in a **territory**, or area of land that it defends. A territory must have plenty of fresh water and enough **prey** to feed all the pack members. In places where several packs live close together, territories may be small. Where packs are spread out, territories can be huge. Wolves mark the **boundaries**, or borders, of their territory with scent. They move along the edges of their territory and leave urine on **scent posts**, or upright markers such as tree stumps. Wolves mark the scent posts constantly, so that other wolves will know to stay out! Wolves have a very strong sense of smell. They use their noses to identify other pack territories and to detect any strange wolves that enter their territory.

Wolves always travel close to a water source, such as a river, because they need to drink a lot of water during the day. Wolf tongues are shaped to lap up large amounts of liquid quickly.

What is a life cycle?

Like all animals, a wolf goes through a series of changes called a **life cycle**. It is born and then grows and changes until it becomes a **mature**, or adult, wolf. Once an animal is mature, it is able to **mate**, or make babies of its own. When the babies are born, a new life cycle begins.

*An animal's **life span** is the length of time it is alive. Wolves in the wild usually live for about eight years. In rare cases, some live up to sixteen years. Captive wolves may live even longer.*

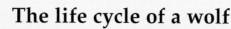

The life cycle of a wolf

A wolf's life cycle begins with the birth of a baby wolf, or **pup**. Pups are usually born in **litters** of two to seven wolves. The pups spend their first weeks of life in a **den**, or shelter, with their mother and littermates. They **nurse**, or feed on their mother's milk.

When they are a month old, the pups meet the rest of their pack. The pack feeds and protects the pups until they can fend for themselves. Some wolves stay with their pack for the rest of their lives, but others leave to join another pack or start a pack of their own.

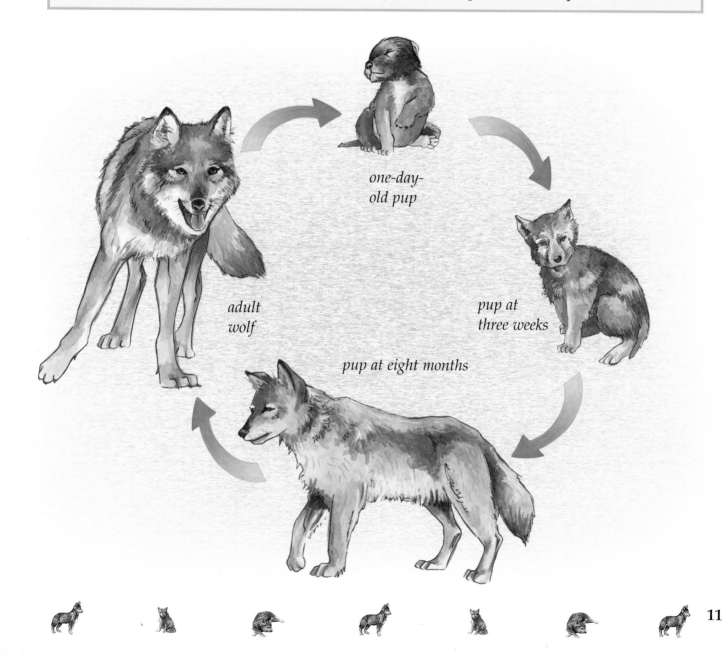

one-day-old pup

pup at three weeks

adult wolf

pup at eight months

A litter is born

Wolf pups are born in the spring. Pups **gestate**, or develop inside their mother's body, for nine weeks before. When the mother wolf is ready to have her babies, she goes into her den, where it is safe and quiet. She gives birth, one at a time, to as many as ten pups.

The tiny pups each weigh about one pound (0.5 kg). They are blind and deaf, and they need their mother to keep them warm with heat from her body. As each pup is born, the mother licks it clean. She guides the pups to the nipples on her underside, where they begin to nurse on milk.

Snuggled up

For the first weeks of their lives, the pups do nothing but sleep and eat. They stay huddled in the den with their mother, who leaves them only to make short trips outside for water and food. She stays close to the pups to protect them and keep them warm with her body heat.

(above) When the pups are two to three weeks old, they can see and hear. The pups have blue eyes when they are born, but their eyes turn gold as they grow.

These small pups are taking their first peek at the world outside their den.

Joining the pack

A mother wolf has led her three-week-old pups out of the den. She lies patiently as they nurse.

This adult female gently lifts a pup with her strong jaws.

When the pups are about a month old, they are ready to leave the den for the first time. They slowly make their way to the entrance, where their mother and the rest of their packmates are waiting. When the pups come out of the den, the other wolves nuzzle and sniff their bodies to greet them and learn their scent.

Team effort

The entire pack now helps look after the pups. The older wolves watch out for **predators**, such as hawks and eagles, which might try to snatch the small pups. While the rest of the pack is away hunting, one adult always stays behind to guard the pups and care for them.

The meeting place

When the pups are eight to ten weeks old, they leave the den for the last time and follow the pack to a **rendezvous site**, or meeting place. This location will be their home for the next few weeks. After that, the pack will choose a new site in their territory about every three weeks.

Baby food

The pups continue to nurse, but they also begin to eat solid food. After a meal, adult wolves return to the rendezvous site and **regurgitate**, or bring up, some food for the pups. The meat is partially digested, so it is easy for the pups to eat. It is also easier for the adults to regurgitate food than to carry whole chunks of meat to the pups.

When adult wolves return from a hunt, the pups eagerly greet them. They lick and nip the corners of an adult's mouth to signal that they want to be fed.

 # Learning to hunt

While their mother hunts with the pack, the pups spend their time playing. They wrestle, run, chase, and stalk one another. These activities keep the pups busy and help them develop the skills and strength they will need to hunt with the rest of the pack.

When the pups are about six months old, the pack stops using a rendezvous site. The pups must now travel with the pack. They also begin to hunt small animals for practice. By the time they are ten months old, most cubs are able to hunt with the pack.

Feeding the gang

Pups must become good hunters in order to help the pack survive. Each pup develops its own skills, such as fast running or quiet stalking, and learns how to hunt as part of a team. The wolves must work together, or they will go hungry. Even experienced packs succeed in catching prey only once in every ten tries. An adult wolf can eat up to 20 pounds (9 kg) of food at one sitting—but it often goes for days without a meal.

Wolves hunt large animals, such as this moose, because they are big enough to feed all the pack members.

The pecking order

The pack does not eat together. First, the alphas eat their fill. Alphas protect the entire pack, so it is important that they stay strong and healthy. The other wolves then get a chance to eat in the order of their **rank**, or place, in the pack (see pages 18-19).

Wolves trot with their heads down low, sniffing the ground to pick up the scent of prey.

Finding their place

Older wolves (above) scuffle to assert themselves, but young wolves (below) play together to determine dominance.

Each wolf has a rank in the pack. The alpha pair is in charge, and every other wolf is ranked below these wolves. Next in command are the **beta** male and female. The lowest ranked wolf is called the **omega**. It is often bullied by the others and is last to eat after a hunt. High-ranking wolves are more **dominant** than the others in the pack. They are large, strong, and **aggressive**. Lower-ranking wolves are **submissive**. They usually back down when challenged.

"Top dog"

Pups of the same age find their place by ranking themselves in their age group. Their rank can change several times before they reach two years of age. By then, each wolf's role in the pack is set.

From their first days in the den, new pups establish their ranking. One pup in the litter may act dominant, but another may soon become even more dominant. Their ranking then changes.

Learning wolf talk

To hunt and live as a pack, wolves must communicate. Pups start learning about **body language**, facial expressions, and wolf sounds when they are first introduced to the pack. Body language sends many different messages. For example, wolves show affection by licking or nipping at the corners of one another's mouths, just as they did when they were pups. They show their rank with the position of their tails and ears. An alpha wolf keeps its tail high and its ears perked up. The omega wolf shows submission by holding its tail between its legs and its ears flat against its head. Other wolves show dominance or submission by keeping their ears and tails between these two positions.

Large pups greet an alpha wolf (center) with low submissive bodies and affectionate sniffs and licks.

Why the sad face?

Wolves also communicate a variety of messages with their faces. Some scientists believe that wolves use as many as 20 different facial expressions! Wolves curl their lips, bare their teeth, narrow their eyes, and even stick out their tongues to show their moods.

Howlin' wolf

The most famous wolf "talk" is the howl. Wolves howl to signal the start of a hunt, to locate another wolf, or to answer another pack's howls. Each wolf has its own voice. Wolves are better at recognizing one another's voices than people are! Their voices are as expressive as their faces. Wolves can change the sound of their howl, and they know how to use echoes to make their pack sound larger than it is. This trick helps them defend their territory against other packs.

Wolves make other noises, too. They snarl, growl, and whimper, just as dogs do.

Ready to mate

When wolves reach adulthood, their **instinct** to mate becomes very strong. Female wolves reach maturity at about two years of age. Male wolves do not become adults until they are three years old.

A mating pair

In a wolf pack, only one pair mates. The mating pair is usually the alpha pair, unless one of the alphas is not interested in mating. In that case, a beta wolf may mate in its place. The mating wolves become very affectionate with each other and spend almost all their time together.

Mating season

Wolves mate only once a year, usually between January and April. This period is called the **mating season**. All adult wolves want to mate at this time, but the alpha pair stops the other wolves from mating by **intimidating**, or scaring, them. Mating season is tense, but life returns to normal when it ends.

Preparing for birth

About six weeks after a female wolf becomes **pregnant**, she starts to prepare for the birth of her pups. First, she selects a site for her den. She chooses a spot that is deep in her pack's territory, where she and her pups will be well protected.

Just the right spot

The site must be sheltered and hidden from view. It also needs to be near water so that the mother can go for a drink without leaving her cubs alone for too long.

These wolves are checking out the site of a new den, which the female will need very soon!

Digging a den

Wolves sometimes make dens in caves or rotten logs, but most dens are **burrows**, or underground holes. A pregnant wolf digs a tunnel between ten and twelve feet long (3-3.5 m). She makes the entrance just big enough to fit her body. She digs one **chamber**, or room, to sleep in and another one at the end of the tunnel, where she will have her pups.

Pitching in

As the day for giving birth draws near, all the pack members help the mother prepare. They bury chunks of meat near the den. This hidden **cache**, or store, of small meals will keep the mother strong while she lives in the den with her pups. After nine weeks of pregnancy, the mother gives birth. With each pup, a new life cycle begins.

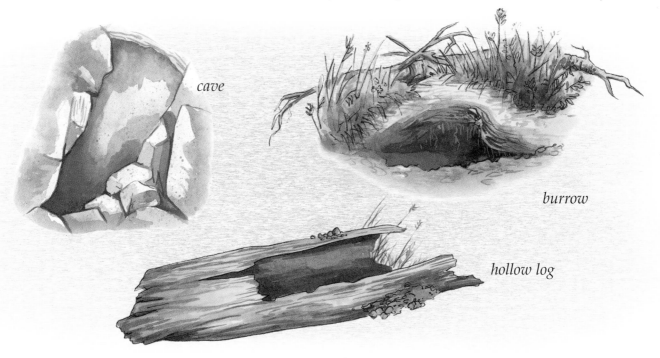

cave

burrow

hollow log

Wolves sometimes use the same den more than once. They may use another animal's abandoned den if it is large enough for the mother and cubs.

Leaving the pack

Many young wolves leave their packs when they become mature. They are called **dispersers**, or lone wolves. Scientists are not sure why lone wolves leave. The wolves may have such a strong need to mate that they go in search of a partner, or they may be forced out of their pack for reasons scientists do not yet know.

On the prowl

A lone wolf has to leave its pack's territory—and stay out! The pack will not let a disperser stick around. Lone wolves must also avoid neighboring wolf territories. They often travel long distances along the boundaries of other packs' territories before they find hunting land that has not been claimed by other wolves.

Starting fresh

Lone wolves live and hunt alone until they find a mate—usually another lone wolf. Together, the two dispersers may become a mating pair. They mark their new territory and stay within its boundaries. When their first litter is born, they start a new pack of their own.

Dangers to wolves

Humans pose the biggest threat to wolves. When European settlers first arrived in North America, there were wolves everywhere! The settlers believed that wolves were a danger to them and to their livestock, so they hunted as many wolves as they could. Governments even put a **bounty** on wolves. People hunted them and received a cash reward for every wolf they killed.

Bad reputation

Today, we know more about wolves and fear them less. Some people, however, still think that wolves are pests. Many farmers and ranchers believe that wolves are a danger to their animals. Some hunters think that wolves kill too many game animals, such as elk and caribou. Scientists disagree with the hunters. They argue that wolf packs actually keep game herds healthy because they hunt the old and sick animals.

Crowded conditions

As cities grow, the natural habitats of wolves are reduced. Wolves are forced into smaller areas where there is not enough food for all of the animals. Many cannot find enough to eat, and they starve. Close living also increases the risk of diseases being passed from wolf to wolf. Sick wolves often spread illnesses to other animals. A single outbreak of disease can kill many wolves, especially if a large number of wolves lives in a small area.

Helping wolves

Today, many people work to protect wolves. In some areas, land has been set aside to create wolf **preserves**, or safe natural habitats for wolf packs. These preserves are open to visits from the public. Scientists also help wolves by constantly learning more about them. By studying the behavior, habitats, food sources, and travel routes of wolves, scientists can help protect these magnificent creatures. They can monitor the health of wolves and fight outbreaks of disease.

Learning more

You can help wolves by learning all you can about them. Wolf websites will give you up-to-date information about wolves and the people who work hard to protect them. These sites will also connect you with wolf-lovers all over the world! Start at www.wolfweb.com, www.wolf.org, or www.canids.org.

When wolves are safe and healthy, they have babies. With each pup, a new life cycle begins!

Glossary

Note: Boldfaced words defined in the book may not appear in the glossary.

aggressive Describing threatening or forceful behavior

body language A way of sending messages through posture, gestures, and facial expressions

boundary A border that divides one area of land from another

bounty A sum of money that is rewarded for killing an animal

dominant Describing an animal that displays controlling or forceful behavior

habitat The natural place where a plant or animal lives

hybrid An animal that is produced by the mating of parents from two species

instinct An animal's natural knowledge or desire

plain A flat area of land with few trees

predator An animal that hunts and eats other animals

pregnant Describing a female that is carrying one or more babies inside her body

submissive Describing an animal that displays timid behavior

tundra The flat, treeless plains of the Arctic

Index

5 6 7 8 9 0 Printed in the U.S.A. 1 0 9 8 7 6 5